It's Just Good Business

The Emergence of Conscious Capitalism & the Practice of Working for Good

Jeff Klein

WORKING FOR
GOOD.
PUBLICATIONS

San Rafael, California

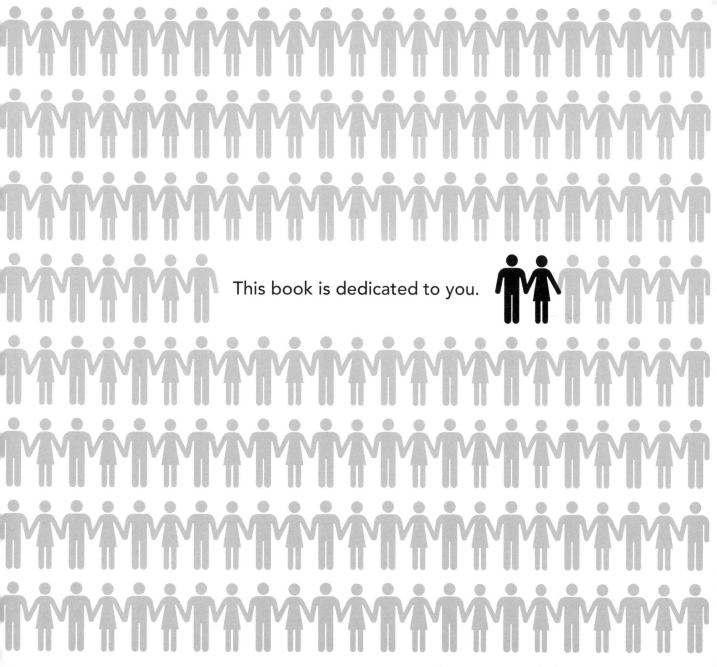

This book is dedicated to you.

"

Work is love made visible.
~ Kahlil Gibran

"

In the beginning...

...was the Big Bang.

Don't worry, I won't take 13+ billion years to tell this story or to get to the point. The point of starting with the Big Bang is to highlight the fact that we are part of an awe-inspiring, emerging process of a scope and scale beyond our comprehension. And while we can aspire to make big things happen, humility is generally healthy.

Though relatively young, the human story is rich, dynamic and ever-unfolding, as we continue to learn, create new tools and evolve our cultures and social systems.

We are an amazingly resilient and adaptable species. Just when it looks like we might be down for the count, we rebound with a fresh perspective, new energy and an innovative approach.

This book explores and celebrates an emerging social and cultural development called Conscious Capitalism.

The book also provides an introduction to the practice of Working for Good - our approach to developing awareness and other skills to increase our ability to embody the principles of Conscious Capitalism and to foster individual and collective flourishing.

Here's to the journey!

 # CONTEXT

Context helps us to orient what follows it. It provides a bridge, an on-ramp, an invitation, a welcoming hand.

Underlying beliefs

These beliefs provide the ground from which the rest of this book springs.

Life wants to live. Human beings, like all life forms, are driven to survive, propagate and perpetuate.

Movement for improvement. We prefer well-being and flourishing over, illness, pain and misery. We are naturally driven to improve our circumstances.

We're part of nature, and it's all one. Life is an ecosystem of interconnected, interrelated and interdependent elements. . . and that includes us!

All for one and one for all. Human beings are social organisms and depend on others to survive, propagate and flourish.

Use everything we've got. Our capacities for sensing, feeling, thinking and reflecting are all essential to our survival and well-being.

Living organisms and natural systems adapt to changing circumstances. As we recognize the life threatening implications of our actions, we learn and develop new approaches and capacities to facilitate our ongoing survival and advancement.

The emergence of Conscious Capitalism® and the practice of Working for Good® are responses to the opportunities to elevate the way human beings orient to life through business and work.

Your work is to discover your work, and then to give yourself to it with all your heart.

~ The Buddha

Where We're Coming From

Working for Good, our business and brand, exists to foster human flourishing.

What We're Doing Here

In this book we articulate a **vision** of an emerging transformation in the way we orient to work, business and life, reflected by the principles of Conscious Capitalism. Then we share **stories** of businesses that embody these principles. Finally, we point to **pathways** you can take to increasingly become a reflection of the vision and a participant in the stories, and to create your own stories

Why We're Doing It

It's our way of responding to the inherent drive to improve our individual and collective ability to survive and flourish.

How We're Doing It

We aspire to foster flourishing through everything we do, including this book, our first book - *Working for Good: Making a Difference While Making a Living*, our radio program and courses under the banner of *It's Just Good Business* at entheos.com, our work with Conscious Capitalism, Inc., our consulting work through Working for Good and our work with BeingHuman.org.

Ultimately, we're doing it by the way we show up in life and at work every day, which is the way any of us do what we do.

Success

Homo sapiens sapiens (that's us, Human Beings) have been a remarkably successful species. From our emergence 200,000 years ago, we have arguably become the dominant (and most dominating) species on the planet.

If life is driven to survive, propagate, perpetuate and flourish, we're doing a pretty good job at it.

From numbers in the low millions 15,000 years ago, living in small, scattered settlements or roaming, our numbers have grown to nearly seven billion, with more than half of our population concentrated in cities.

In the past 50,000 years our life expectancy has more than doubled to nearly seventy years.

In tribal societies of early humans, nearly a third of adult males died by violence inflicted by another human being. Now, even with periodic mass killings, the percentage of death by violence inflicted by another human being is infinitesimal.

We have gone from being self-propelled or carried by animals to whizzing through space. From sending smoke signals to communicate to nearby neighbors, to instantly connecting across the globe.

Bottom Line: We've come a long way in 200,000 years! And in the modern age, business plays a primary role in driving our accelerating and expanding success – deepening our knowledge, increasing our technological capacity to transform the world and adding to the useful goods and services available to us.

At a Price: Unintended Consequences & Collateral Damage

However, our success has come at a price, and this price may be reaching a point at which it threatens our survival and undermines our individual and collective well-being.

Our scientific understanding and related technological developments have increased our power to transform natural resources into energy and products. We organize vast numbers of people in a global economic web that facilitates mind-boggling productivity. And we expect, demand and consume at ever-increasing levels.

At the same time, and arguably on account of our success, we deplete natural resources, degrade natural systems and foster stress and disease for ourselves.

Obesity. Unemployment. Soaring health care costs. Epidemic stress and ADD. Alienation at work. Water shortages. Soil depletion. Bank bailouts. Mortgage foreclosures. Rampant PTSD. Toxic chemicals soup surrounding us....

To a meaningful extent, business and the economic system reward financial performance at the expense of performance in other domains, such as social behavior (people are often treated as expendable resources) or impact on ecosystems (considered "externalities" and often disregarded), and allow people to abdicate responsibility in these other domains.

You get the point, and we trust we don't need to beat it home.

It is interesting to note that pigs don't sh–t where they sleep. Only humans do.

9

"

The times they are a-changin.

~ Bob Dylan

"

Recognition

The good news: we are recognizing the impact and implications of human activity on ourselves, our communities and the natural systems and resources on which our lives and businesses depend.

We recognize the power of human beings, through business and otherwise, to threaten or enhance our individual and collective survival and well-being. And we recognize an emerging course adjustment, in which we shift from a short-term to a long-term orientation and from crony Capitalism to Conscious Capitalism, with life-enhancing approaches to business and to our relationship with natural ecosystems.

The rapid growth of the Conscious Capitalism community, including participation from CEOs of large public companies is a powerful indication of the emergence.

Another sign of the emergence – (at the time of publication of this book. . .)

> *558 small to medium sized companies with $3.35 B in revenue in 60 industries have become Certified B Corporations – a new type of corporation, which "uses the power of business to solve social and environmental problems. B Corps meet comprehensive and transparent social and environmental performance standards; meet higher legal accountability standards; and actively build business constituency for good business."*

More signs to come...

Perhaps the safest prediction we can make about the future is that it will surprise us.

~ George Leonard

A Final Word on Context

Something is going on. We feel it. We long for it. We call for it. What exactly it is and how it will unfold, who knows?

I'm reminded of a traditional Taoist story that reminds us to not to be so certain of anything we presume to be so. (This is a modified version of the story): *One day the farmer's only horse broke out of the corral and ran away. Upon hearing the news, the farmer's neighbors came to his house to see for themselves. They said, "Oh, what bad luck!" To which the farmer replied, "Maybe it is, maybe it isn't."*

Within a week the horse returned, accompanied by a beautiful wild stallion, which the farmer and his son quickly corralled. Once again, upon hearing the news, the neighbors came to see for themselves. This time they proclaimed, "Oh, what good luck!" The farmer replied, "Maybe it is, maybe it isn't."

While he was working to break the wild stallion, the farmer's son was thrown against a fence and broke his leg. True to form, the neighbors gathered round to console the farmer with "Oh, what bad luck!" And once again, the farmer replied, "Maybe it is, maybe it isn't."

During this period of time in China, two rival warlords were at war with each other. The warlord ruling over the Taoist farmer's village, one of the two combatants, visited the village to conscript young men to fight in the war. When his men came to take the farmer's son, they found him unable to walk, and left him behind, taking the beautiful stallion instead. The farmer's neighbors didn't know quite what to say. The farmer smiled.

Let's envision flourishing for all and act with purpose and passion, while maintaining an expanded perspective and a sense of humor!

 DEFINITIONS

"We need to recall that we do not just make words up or learn them in school, or ever have them fully under control. Words, like angels, are powers which have invisible power over us. They are personal presences which have whole mythologies: genders, genealogies (etymologies concerning origins and creations), histories, and vogues; and their own guarding, blaspheming, creating, and annihilating effects."

~ James Hillman

Hillman's point: let's take our words seriously and recognize that they have significant effects on us and implications between us.

What a word means to us informs the way we relate to the thing it represents and to the way we relate to each other.

So let's get down (or move up) to business... and define our terms, with care.

"

The greatest discovery of my age is that men can change their circumstances by changing the attitude of their mind.

~William James

Definition: Conscious Awareness

Conscious Awareness is a process of recognizing what is going on inside and out, the effects of decisions and actions, and the interaction between a complex array of factors and forces. It is seeing our seeing, observing our thoughts and recognizing our feelings and the effect they have on us, others and our surroundings.

Much of what occurs within and between us is unconscious. That is, it happens without our Conscious Awareness that is it happening, much as our heart beats whether we notice it or not. This is good, as tracking everything that is going on would clearly overload, overwhelm and paralyze us. But much of our unconscious behavior – following social and cultural programs set in place decades or millennia ago – often limits and inhibits us from being more effective.

Conscious Awareness supports us to be present with the people and circumstances we are facing in the moment, rather than ruminating about the past, projecting into the future or otherwise being carried away by sensations, feelings, thoughts, and intuitions.

Conscious Awareness is a meta skill – one that enhances the performance of other skills. It functions much as a mirror functions for a dancer – reflecting position and movement, providing feedback to facilitate adjustment. We cultivate awareness so we can reflect and respond to challenges and opportunities rather than just react to them.

Go to page 77 if you'd like to check out a simple awareness practice.

> *Capitalism is the most successful form of human social cooperation ever created.*
>
> *~Ed Freeman*

Definition: Capitalism

Capitalism is the socioeconomic system based on the principles of property rights, rule of law, voluntary exchange, wealth creation and entrepreneurial initiative. Business (defined in more detail on the next page) is the human activity and form of social organization embodying and operating under these principles.

Ultimately, Capitalism is a system based on the creation and accumulation of (financial, social, intellectual, relational, technological...) capital to serve individual, group and collective human survival, propagation and flourishing.

*Business is a creative and therefore spiritual endeavor.
Great entrepreneurs enter the field of business in
the same way great artists enter the field of art.
With their business creation, entrepreneurs express
their desire for self-realization, evolutionary passion
for self-fulfillment, and creative vision of a new world.
The entrepreneur's business is their artwork.
Thecreation of business is as creative as any creation
in art. In fact, building a business may be the
most creative human activity.*

~ Yasuhiko Kimura

Definition: Business

Business is a form of human social organization: people getting together for a purpose; to do something together and to deliver value to themselves and others.

Business is an outlet for creative expression, a structure and process for turning ideas into products and services and a vehicle for creating wealth – financial, material, intellectual, technological, social, even spiritual – for individuals and society.

In the simplest sense, "good business" = making money by delivering products and services that people want, creating value for others through life-enhancing products and processes.

Business is a human endeavor and can be a path for individual and collective learning, growth and development.

By cultivating Conscious Awareness and other essential skills at work, we can create more human, resilient and life-enhancing businesses.

*When you tug at a single thing in nature,
you find it attached to the rest of the world.*

~ John Muir

Definition: Ecosystem

Eco (oikos) is the Greek word for word for home, house, habitat and the root for both ecology (study or knowledge of the home) and economy (management of the home).

The ecosystem is how the home works: all of the components interconnecting to form a coherent network of physical elements and living organisms that is greater than the sum of its parts and reliably self-sustaining.

Ecosystems usually have discreet physical boundaries and are themselves components of larger and larger ecosystems.

Individual human beings can be understood as natural biological ecosystems. We are composed of trillions of interconnected cells, organs and functional systems. And there are somewhere between 500 and 1000 species of bacteria living in our guts and on our skin, and more than ten times as many bacteria cells in and on our bodies than there are "human" cells.

A business can also be constructively understood as an ecosystem, comprised of and dependent on all of the interconnected elements necessary to its endeavor, including biological organisms, social networks, technological systems, materials, products and the ecosystems it inhabits that affect and are affected by it.

THE EMERGENCE OF
CONSCIOUS CAPITALISM

The Vision

Everyone can flourish and we are capable of creating businesses and economies that elevate humanity. The emergence of Conscious Capitalism reflects and fuels this vision.

About Conscious Capitalism

Conscious Capitalism is an idea, a movement, an approach to conducting business and a nonprofit organization (Conscious Capitalism, Inc.) dedicated to advancing all of these, through transformative thinking, programs, events, and communities of inquiry.

Conscious Capitalism is an adaptive improvement on Capitalism, which, itself, is an inherently effective system for facilitating global-scale cooperation, innovation and wealth creation. It is an upgraded Operating System for business that reflects a recognition of interdependence and the essential role of natural systems to human survival and well-being. It represents a shift in orientation from "I, me, mine" to "I and we, me and us, mine and all of ours."

Conscious Capitalism has its roots in the earliest corporations, established hundreds of years ago, with limited charters focused on providing a specific service to the community, such as building a bridge, or some other large public work. The tradition of business in service to community is embodied in the foundational documents and histories of late nineteenth century companies like Johnson & Johnson and Avon, which were explicitly created to address social needs and to serve people. Dozens of companies started in the late nineteen sixties through the nineteen seventies, emerging out of the social movements of the sixties, carry on this tradition and pioneered the philosophy of Conscious Capitalism.

Today, Conscious Capitalism, Inc. is experiencing substantial and rapidly expanding interest in the Conscious Capitalism philosophy and community.

"Conscious businesses will help evolve our culture and social systems so that billions of people can flourish, leading lives infused with passion, purpose, love and creativity; a world of freedom, harmony, prosperity and compassion."

~ from the Conscious Capitalism Credo

Conscious Capitalism: Applied to Business

The rubber meets the road with Conscious Capitalism as it is applied to business. The four principles guiding and underlying a business that practices Conscious Capitalism are:

1. **Higher Purpose**: Recognizing that every business has a purpose that includes, but is more than, making money. By focusing on its Higher Purpose, a business inspires, engages and energizes its stakeholders.

2. **Stakeholder Orientation**: Recognizing interdependent nature of life and the human foundations and business, a business needs to create value with and for its various stakeholders (customers, employees, vendors, investors, communities, etc.). Like the life forms in an ecosystem, healthy stakeholders lead to a healthy business system.

3. **Conscious Leadership**: Human social organizations are created and guided by leaders – people who see a path and inspire others to travel along the path. Conscious Leaders understand and embrace the Higher Purpose of business and focus on creating value for and harmonizing the interests of the business' stakeholders. They recognize the integral role of culture and purposefully cultivate Conscious Culture.

4. **Conscious Culture**: This is the ethos – the values, principles, practices – underlying the social fabric of a business, which permeates the atmosphere of a business and connects the stakeholders to each other and to the purpose, people and processes that comprise the company.

*"People must be motivated by a deeper cause.
I believe that people don't come to work to earn money for
themselves and the company. They come to work because the product
does something worthwhile, and this is what inspires people."*

~ Bill George

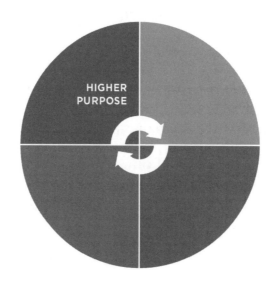

The Power of Purpose

One of the things that sets human beings apart from other animals is our capacity and need for meaning and purpose in our lives.

Purpose is an activating, motivating and animating force. It moves us to get up in the morning, sustains us when times get tough and serves as a guiding star when we stray off course.

Purposeful people build purposeful companies. And purposeful people make an impact through whatever their work or role may be.

While making money is among the purposes of a business, every business has a purpose beyond making money. When a business is deeply rooted in its deeper purpose, its stakeholders – founders and leaders, employees, customers and others – feel a deep, meaningful connection to the business, which contributes to sustainable and resilient relationships.

Purpose inspires and connects, like an energetic or electric glue.

"We need red blood cells to live
(the same way a business needs profits to live),
but the purpose of life is more than to make red
blood cells (the same way the purpose of business is
more than simply to generate profits)."

~ Ed Freeman

Articulating Purpose

The Dallas-based marketing agency MEplusYOU employs a powerful process for facilitating articulation of a brand's, product's, business' or other organization's purpose. Beginning with core or underlying beliefs, the process generates an expression of WHY the organization exists, HOW it fulfills its purpose and WHAT, specifically, it does. Below is the Purpose Proposition for Conscious Capitalism, Inc.

Evolving Purpose

Tony Hsieh, the visionary entrepreneur largely responsible for building Zappos from an early stage, start-up to a billion dollar company in five years, before selling controlling interest to Amazon.com, passionately articulates the evolution of Zappos' (and, to a meaningful extent, his own) purpose during the development of the business.

Phase 1: **Selling shoes** - In the beginning, Zappos was in the business of selling shoes.

Phase 2: **Delivering service** - After a couple years, Tony and the Zappos team recognized that what set them apart and delighted their customers was their unusual, exceptional and often outrageous service - an expression of their playful culture.

Phase 3: **Delivering happiness** - As the business evolved, it became clear that Zappos' culture was the heart of the business, and this culture was essentially based in delivering happiness to its customers and team members. With this recognition came the next iteration of Zappos' purpose.

Phase 4: **Building healthy communities** - Relatively recently, as the Zappos leadership team turned their attention to building a new corporate headquarters in Las Vegas in a way that reflected their purpose and supported their culture, they realized they had an even deeper purpose - to create healthy, thriving communities. This realization led Tony to activate The Downtown Project, independently of Zappos, a $350 million project to revitalize downtown Las Vegas, integrating the new Zappos headquarters into a thriving urban community.

As Tony and Zappos' story reflects, human beings and companies learn, grow and develop over time. As our purpose evolves, so do we. And as we develop, so does our purpose and that of our enterprises.

"In a healthy, complex, evolving, and self-adapting system, the harmony of interests between stakeholders proves to be far more important and resilient than the various perceived conflicts of interest between them"

~ John Mackey, co-founder & co-CEO, Whole Foods Market, co-founder, Conscious Capitalism, Inc.

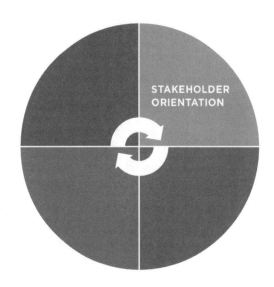

The Implications of Interdependence

Underlying the stakeholder orientation of Conscious Capitalism, with a focus on creating value for all of the stakeholders in a business, is the recognition of the implications of interdependence.

In our modern age, a financial crisis in one part of the world or one sector of the economy creates ripples throughout the global economy. Natural disasters release toxic wastes that threaten communities in distant lands. Social unrest in one country or continent spills into neighboring countries and distant continents. Technological advances in a single garage transform the way billions of people communicate with each other and the possibilities for how we live our lives.

A paycheck and benefits were once sufficient to satisfy employees. Creating jobs and paying taxes were once sufficient for satisfying communities. Generating high ROI was once sufficient for investors. As our technologies, social-economic systems, scientific understandings and daily lives become more complex, so too do our brains and our perspectives.

Key stakeholders in the ecosystem of business increasingly demand that businesses recognize interdependence and consider the effects of their products, services and processes on people and natural ecosystems, both now and in the future. They increasingly expect that companies have an explicit social purpose that drives their business. And they expect companies to create value and serve society, beyond the goods and services they deliver.

In the emerging Conscious Capitalism economy, making money requires more than focusing on making money, but on elevating the health of the entire business ecosystem.

*"When the Master governs, the people
are hardly aware that he exists. ...
The Master doesn't talk, he acts.
When his work is done, the people say
"Amazing: we did it, all by ourselves!"*

~ Lao Tzu, Tao Te Ching

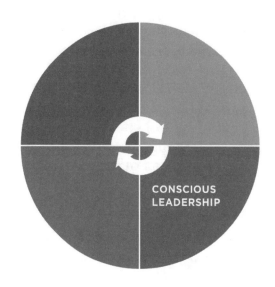

Conscious Leadership

Leadership is a process of inspiring and engaging others to move in a direction to accomplish something together. Leaders are people who activate and sustain this process. A Conscious Leader is someone who leads with Conscious Awareness.

Conscious Leaders recognize the higher purpose and interdependence of the stakeholders in their business and focus on fulfilling the purpose, creating value for all of the stakeholders and cultivating a culture that supports this process.

Conscious Leaders and conscious leadership are essential to the ongoing learning, growth and development of an organization, and of the people who comprise its corpus (the word corporation comes from Latin root *corpus* or body. To incorporate is to embody).

Leadership is a function and role that can and must be broadly distributed throughout an organization, dynamically changing with context. Conscious Leaders know when it is appropriate for others to take the lead - even if for only a "moment" - and they cultivate the awareness and other capacities of leadership in others.

"If your actions inspire others to dream more, learn more, do more and become more, you are a leader."

~ John Quincy Adams

"Culture eats strategy for lunch."

~ Peter Drucker

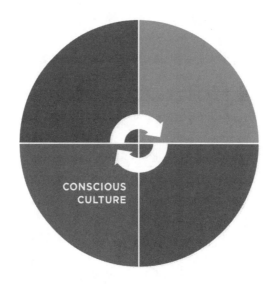

Conscious Culture

Culture encompasses the array of behaviors and beliefs expected and accepted by members of a social group for themselves and other members of the group. Culture includes shared beliefs and values, rules of conduct and rituals. It is a kind of collective programming that distinguishes one group from another, and members of a group from those of other groups.

A Conscious Culture is one that activates individual and collective reflection and explicit articulation of what we see or wonder as we reflect, fostering ongoing learning, growth and development for group members and the group as a whole.

A Conscious Culture is alive. While it provides the same kind of sustained identity and social connective tissue as any other culture, it is dynamic. It fosters innovation and adaptation, and calls for people to deeply engage with each other and with the group's purpose and process.

A Conscious Culture in business fosters embodied commitment to the company's purpose, creating value for the interdependent stakeholders and elevating the entire stakeholder ecosystem.

Conscious Leaders catalyze Conscious Culture by applying and cultivating the practice of Conscious Awareness for themselves, their team members and between the company and its stakeholders.

Culture is not created by one person or even one team. Culture is a spirit of values that you believe in and you walk it, talk it, breathe it and live it.

~ Colleen Barrett

Conscious Culture Questions

There is no magic yardstick that measures and compares levels of Conscious Awareness or degrees of Conscious Culture. These are dynamic attributes that ebb and flow. But with ongoing attention and practice, overall levels of awareness and functioning continually elevate. Here are some specific questions to consider when assessing a company's culture:

What do we care about? What do we value? How do we treat each other? How do we treat our stakeholders – our customers, vendors and others?

Do we have an explicit understanding the factors we consider when making significant decisions that may affect one or more of our stakeholders?

Are roles, responsibilities, authority and accountability clear?

When people have issues with other people in our workplace, do we address difficult issues openly and directly, with awareness, compassion and clarity, or do we gossip about them or undermine each other? Can we agree to disagree? Can we opt out of emotional conversations if we choose to?

Is power exercised explicitly or implicitly? Are people direct and respectful with each other or otherwise?

Do we feel as though we continue to learn, grow and develop together?

Do we feel alive? Do we have fun and celebrate together?

When the dust settles from this Armageddon, the only companies left standing are going to be the ones that stand for something that improves people's lives.

~ Roy Spence

Closing Thoughts on Conscious Capitalism

Conscious Capitalism represents a paradigm shift - a reorientation of the way we look at and conduct business.

It creates more sustainable, resilient companies, but it is more than sustainability.

Conscious Capitalists and conscious businesses embrace their responsibility to society, but Conscious Capitalism is much more than Corporate Social Responsibility, which tends to be an "add on" to the old business paradigm, which focuses primarily on profit.

Conscious Capitalism is dynamic and the people who embrace and embody it are committed to their ongoing learning, growth and development. This means that Conscious Capitalism will continue to evolve and emerge and, perhaps in our lifetimes, all Capitalism will be Conscious Capitalism, as it becomes clear to all that it is simply a better way of doing business for all involved. It truly is just good business, in every respect.

 STORIES

Bringing the Vision to Life

The idea and principles of Conscious Capitalism and the orientation to business, work and life it represents are far from fantasy, but a rapidly emerging reality.

On the following pages you will find stories of companies and the people who comprise them that are bringing these ideas and principles to life every day, in many ways.

These are but a handful (or two) of countless companies and people who live the idea of Conscious Capitalism every day.

- ❑ Life is good
- ❑ Zappos
- ❑ Whole Foods Market
- ❑ Pencils of Promise
- ❑ The Motley Fool
- ❑ The Container Store
- ❑ Pantheon Enterprises
- ❑ Bamboo Sushi

For each company how they bring the four pillars of Conscious Capitalism to life and one or more of the principles or best practices they are especially masterful in embodying. Without exception, they all embrace their company's higher purpose and focus on creating value for all of their stakeholders. Their leaders are conscious - dedicated to advancing the company's purpose, serving and creating values for it's stakeholders, and cultivating a vibrant, conscious culture.

lifeisgood.com

Life is good

Origins: In the Summer of 1994, Bert and John Jacobs were selling T-shirts on college campuses, sleeping in their van. Ever the optimists, one day they made 48 T-shirts featuring Jake, whose smiling face embodied the brothers' own positive spirit and the three simple words that soon became the company's name: *Life is good*. The shirts sold immediately and the company was off and running, fast becoming a widely admired apparel and lifestyle brand.

Purpose: Spreading the power of optimism.

Stakeholder Orientation: *Life is good* is passionately committed to spreading optimism throughout its ecosystem, which increasingly encompasses the human community at large.

Leadership: Co-founder and CEO Bert Jacobs leads as he lives, with passion, purpose and playfulness. This spirit pervades the company. His brother John, Chief Creative Optimist, continues to pioneer the creative expression of the spirit of optimism.

Culture: Based on the mantra "Do what you like. Like what you do." Built on three values: simplicity, humility and a sense of humor. Live and work with appreciation and spread the spirit to others. Work hard and play hard.

Key Initiatives/Best Practices:

Playmakers: *Life is good* blurs the line between a for-profit and nonprofit by infusing its social mission to help kids in need into everything it does. Every part of the business and every consumer touch point is used to support and further the mission of its nonprofit action arm, *Life is good* Playmakers, to help kids overcome poverty, violence and illness through the healing power of play.

Community Engagement: *Life is good* produces a one-of-a-kind annual fundraising festival combining music, interactive art and backyard games for all ages. Every participant is encouraged to raise funds for the *Life is good* Playmakers, and since 2010, more than $1.7 million has been raised to help kids in need. The festival is one of many community events and platforms for engaging *Life is good* friends and fans in the work of the Playmakers.

The *Life is good* website is a community engagement platform that integrate the company's purpose, products and social mission to help kids.

Zappos!.com

zappos.com

Origins: Frustrated when he couldn't find a pair of shoes that worked for him while shopping in 1999, and finding no good web site selling shoes, Nick Swinmurn started shoesite.com, with aspirations of becoming the Amazon.com of shoes. Soon thereafter Tony Hsieh, who had sold his first company, LinkExchange, to Microsoft for $265 million, invested in Nick's business and eventually stepped in as CEO. They changed the name, and got to work. The rest, is history.

Purpose: To live and Deliver Wow.

Stakeholder Orientation: Cultivate healthy happy people - customers, employees and communities. Happiness as a business model.

Leadership: Focused on embodying the company's core values (by themselves and their team) and cultivating a culture of happiness.

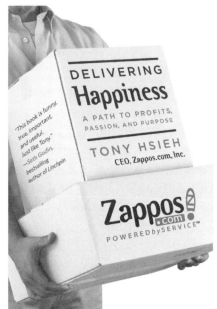

Culture: Zappos Family Core Values

- Deliver WOW Through Service
- Embrace and Drive Change
- Create Fun and A Little Weirdness
- Be Adventurous, Creative, and Open-Minded
- Pursue Growth and Learning
- Build Open & Honest Relationships With Communication
- Build a Positive Team and Family Spirit
- Do More With Less
- Be Passionate and Determined
- Be Humble

Key Initiatives/Best Practices:

Annual Culture Book: A combination of all of Zappos employees' ideas about the culture to distribute to employees, prospective employees, business partners, tour guests and customers.

Delivering Happiness: First it was a book. Then it was a bus tour. Now it's a Movement. The DH Movement grows with every happy person that joins our community. And with all of us working towards the greater goal, together we're nudging the world towards passion, purpose and a happier place.

wholefoodsmarket.com

Origins: John Mackey and Rene Lawson were two young people, passionate about natural foods and looking for a fun way to pay their bills. They started a natural food store called Safer Way. A year later, in 1980, they joined forces with Craig Weller and Mark Skiles, owners of Clarksville Natural Grocery, and launched the first Whole Foods Market, which has become one of the leading natural food and organic supermarkets in the United States.

Purpose: Whole Foods, Whole People, Whole Planet.

Stakeholder Orientation: Create value for all stakeholders, with the customer being the first priority and team members a close second.

Leadership: Co-CEOs John Mackey and Walter Robb lead a team-based organization, with authority/responsibility/accountability distributed throughout the system. Teams within stores, stores within regions and regions within the country have great autonomy within a general framework. Values and team process drive decisions.

48

Culture: Team-based culture, focused on empowerment and ongoing learning, growth and development, and based on seven Core Values.

1. Selling the highest quality natural & organic products available
2. Satisfying & delighting our customers
3. Supporting team member happiness & excellence
4. Creating wealth through profits & growth
5. Caring about our communities & our environment
6. Creating ongoing win-win partnerships with our suppliers
7. Promoting the health of our stakeholders through healthy eating education

Key Initiatives/Best Practices: a few of many!

Whole Planet Foundation: Provides micro-loans to women in communities where WFM sources products. To date, more than 200,000 recipients, more than $29 million in loans, more than 1.2 million people supported.

Whole Kids Foundation: Dedicated to improving children's nutrition and wellness with the goal of ending the childhood obesity epidemic.

Team Member Health Savings Accounts: Support and encourage Team Members to care for themselves.

Appreciations: Meetings at all levels - from store teams to the board - close with appreciations.

 **PENCILS OF PROMISE** pencilsofpromise.org

Origins: Backpacking in India in 2005, Adam Braun asked a small boy who approached him with and outstretched hand, "What do you want most in the world?" The boy's response, "A pencil." This simple answer inspired Adam to hand out thousands of pencils to children in similar circumstances and, ultimately, to launch Pencils of Promise with $25 in 2008. Since then Pencils for Promise has built dozens of schools in disadvantaged communities around the world. The promise and process continue to build.

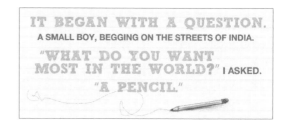

Purpose: Empower the world.
One child, one pencil at a time.

Stakeholder Orientation: Pencils of Promise is a "for purpose" organization, driven by its commitment to deliver quality education to the more than 61 million children around the world who do not have access.

Photo © Bryce Eriksen

Leadership: Adam leads an inspired team of young professionals dedicated to catalyzing a global movement to fulfil the organization's purpose.

Culture: Inspired by purpose. Fueled by passion. Sustained through deep commitment, the energy of accomplishment and the joy of service.

Key Initiatives/Best Practices:

For Purpose: Everything Pencils for Promise does is directed towards advancing its purpose, and its purpose provides the foundation for all decisions and actions. Adam and his team believe that any organization, for profit or not for profit, can generate extraordinary results if they are grounded in and engage their stakeholders through their purpose.

Partnerships: Pencils of Promise collaborates with a wide array of corporate and other organizational partners, to support the building of schools, delivery of educational materials and ongoing outreach and resource development. Inspired by purpose, and recognizing the system-wide effects of educating the most disenfranchised, partners are participating in a global ecosystem in which Pencils of Promise is an expanding node.

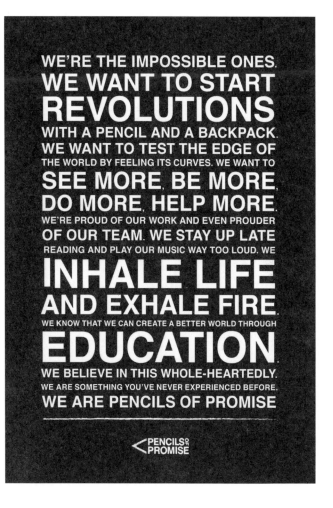

 **The Motley Fool**
To Educate, Amuse & Enrich™ fool.com

Origins: The Motley Fool started in 1993 when brothers Tom and David Gardner pursued their passion to educate, amuse, and enrich everyday investors. As for the name…in Shakespeare, the court jester (AKA, the fool) was the one person who could speak the truth to the King without having his head lopped off.

Purpose: To help the world invest – better.

Stakeholder Orientation: Every year, The Motley Fool helps millions of individual investors build long-term wealth through patient, business-focused investing. The company is a tireless champion for ethics, transparency and accountability in the finance industry and, as an Employee-First organization, also aims to help all 250 employees invest their time, resources, and skills to lead balanced and fulfilling lives.

Leadership: The Gardners embrace the principles of Conscious Capitalism as guiding tenets of The Motley Fool and, when investing, seek out businesses that uphold those same values.

52

Culture: The Foolish culture is based on these core values.

1. Collaborate - Do great things together.
2. Innovate - Search for a better solution. Then top it!
3. Fun - Revel in your work.
4. Honest - Make us proud.
5. Competitive- Play fair, play hard, play to win.
6. Motley – We all bring our own unique value to the Fool.

Key Initiatives/Best Practices:

A True Work/Life Balance: The Motley Fool understands the hectic, 24/7 dynamic of the current workplace and encourages employees to take off as much time as they need, when they need it. The company also has a full-time Wellness Fool who works with employees during office hours leading exercise classes and even meditation to help them stay healthy, happy, and productive.

Follow Your Passion: Word has it, there's only one Chief Collaboration Officer in the US and he's at The Motley Fool. The CCO joins the company's Spirit Guide and 14-person-strong Culture Club department in helping employees work together and pursue their passions—which often leads to new, exciting roles in the company and beyond.

The Container Store®
The Original Storage and Organization Store®

standfor.containerstore.com

Origins: On July 1, 1978, Kip Tindell (Chairman & CEO), Garrett Boone (Chairman Emeritus), and John Mullen (Architect) opened a retail store in Dallas offering a mix of products devoted to helping people simplify their lives.

Purpose: Improve quality of life through the gift of organization.

Stakeholder Orientation: The Container Store explicitly puts their employees first. They take great care of employees who take great care of customers. Ultimately shareholders benefit more from this approach to business than if the company focused myopically on shareholders.

Similarly, TCS treats its suppliers as true partners generating deep collaboration and great loyalty.

Leadership: CEO Kip Tindell and his executive team, comprised principally of women, including President Melissa Reiff and Chief Merchandising Officer Sharon Tindell, live by the Golden Rule and by the company's Foundation Principles™, which reflect their business philosophy and approach.

Culture: The Container Store is proud of its "yummy culture" filled with an Air of Excitement! It all starts with hiring great people, training and treating them well.

Key Initiatives/Best Practices:

Foundation Principles:
- 1 Great Person = 3 Good People
- Communication IS Leadership
- Fill the other guy's basket to the brim. Making money then becomes an easy proposition.
- The Best SELECTION, SERVICE & PRICE
- Intuition does not come to an unprepared mind. You need to train before it happens.
- Man In The Desert Selling
- Air of Excitement

Employee Development. The Container Store offers more than 263 hours of formal training for full-time employees in their first year, compared to the industry average of about eight hours. They experience less than 10% annual turnover compared to retail industry averages of 100% and more.

Commitment to Community: The Container Store gives back to the community with a focus on supporting nonprofits that promote women's and children's well-being and health.

 **Sustain Better Life.**  sustainbetterlife.com

PANTHEON ENTERPRISES, INC.

Origins: When her father died unexpectedly in 1997, Laura Roberts, avid environmentalist, elementary school teacher and administrator, decided to preserve his legacy - a small, chemical company that made green cleaners, started in a garage in the mid-1980s. From that decision, Laura began a true hero's journey, which dynamically continues fifteen years later.

Purpose: Revolutionize the industrial chemical industry by replacing widely-used hazardous products & processes with technologies that are 1) high-performance, 2) safe and 3) a significant improvement to our customers' bottom line.

Stakeholder Orientation: To be a magnet for innovative technologies, loyal customers and outstanding, collaborative people who have a passion for making a difference.

Leadership: A serious student of everything she puts her mind to, committed to ongoing development of leadership capacity – for herself and her colleagues – Laura has taken Birthing of Giants Program at MIT's Sloan School and the Stagen Institute's year-long Integral Leadership Program.

A mother of three, Laura travels tirelessly for the business and is training for a triathlon at the time of this writing. She aims to excel and leads by example.

Culture: Pantheon aims high - to transform a powerful industry with substantial impact on the health of people and planet. To pursue this mission requires healthy, passionate people with drive, persistence and great skill. A culture of excellence, collaboration and innovation forms the foundation of their success.

Key Initiatives/Best Practices:

Pantheon Products: For more than a decade, Pantheon Enterprises has been helping companies and governments remove dangerous hexavalent chromium from painting processes. Pantheon improves machine performance through its innovative metalworking fluids, offers high-performance weapon care products, and provides innovative industrial cleaning solutions utilizing environmentally safe technologies.

Technologies developed by Pantheon Enterprises are bringing direct, environmentally responsible solutions to all aspects of business, solving complex problems and helping to build a socially progressive business community. The company's solutions minimize environmental impact while maximizing effectiveness creating the rare safe technologies that are both cost and performance effective.

Changing perspectives: Key to the company's success is the ability to shift client's perspectives from looking at unit cost to considering use cost, and to recognizing the positive bottom line implications of the shift.

BAMBOO SUSHI

sustainable. delectable. possible.

bamboosushi.com

Origins: Kristofor Lofgren grew up in Berkeley, California, raised principally by his father, who was not overly fond of cooking. At a young age, Kristofor developed an appreciation for restaurants and good food. In his early 20s, when he invested in a sushi restaurant whose founder had no real vision, Kristofor took over and decided to pursue his passion for making a difference and restoring ecosystems through sushi, and created the first certified, sustainable sushi restaurant in the world.

Purpose: Change the world by connecting people to each other and ecosystems through food.

Stakeholder Orientation: "So go our vendors, so we go." "Our employees are our story." "We create Wow! Experiences for our guests and support them to transcend time." Bamboo sushi is the first restaurant to collaborate with some of the world's largest ecosystem-focused NGOs.

Leadership: Kristofor observes that "If I am not growing, we're dying as a company." And, "We lead by embodying our values."

Culture: Based on seven core values.

1. Go Above & Beyond, For Our Guests…and Each Other
2. Sharing & Empowerment.
3. Kaizen. Each day we do better than the day before.
4. Create Success for Others.
5. Be Adaptable.
6. Be Proactive.
7. Have Fun.

Key Initiatives/Best Practices:

Marine Protection: Donated $250,000 to The Nature Conservancy to create and fund The Berry Islands Marine Preserve, a vital ecosystem in the Bahamas, to be studied for its regenerative impacts.

Partnerships: Marine Stewardship Council, Monterey Bay Aquarium, Blue Ocean Institute, Salmon Nation, KidSafe Seafood, and the Green Restaurant Association.

Educating Guests and Others: Through signage in the restaurants, videos, events and other vehicles. "Education is essential for advancing the movement to preserve and regenerate the oceans."

The universe is made of stories, not atoms.

~ Muriel Rukeyser

Closing Reflection on Stories

Tuning in to the mainstream media and popular perceptions, it's easy to believe that we are going to hell in a hand basket, so to speak. But if we tune into the amazing, inspiring things countless companies and the people who comprise them are doing to create new stories, in the context of the big over arching story of the emergence of Conscious Capitalism, it's just as easy to feel life-enhancing energy and to recognize that something profound, powerful and positive is emerging, expressing itself through millions of individuals and thousands of companies, throughout the world.

The preceding profiles represent a handful of countless companies, their leaders and stakeholders who are creating inspiring new stories every day.

Each of us can be part of an almost infinite number of these stories, through where and what we buy, where we invest, where and how we work. By doing so we inform and influence their ongoing emergence.

And we can create new ones ourselves.

The next time you want to complain about the state of the world, consider this...

"Criticize by creating."

~ Michelangelo

 PATHWAYS

Be the change you want to see in the world.

~ Mahatma Gandhi

To know and not to do is not to know.

~ Wang Yangming

Knowing others is intelligence;
knowing yourself is true wisdom.
Mastering others is strength;
mastering yourself is true power.

~ Lao Tzu, Tao Te Ching

If you want to be the change, do the work!

The Process is the Product

"The Process is the Product" is our motto and at the core of the Practice of Working for Good.

By "The Process is the Product" we mean that what we create through our businesses reflects the way we conduct ourselves in business. If we want our work to be meaningful and fulfilling and our businesses to be resilient, sustainable and successful over the long-term, then we need to treat ourselves, each other and the world around us with care and respect.

Becoming more human at work and building business cultures that foster flourishing takes sustained attention and effort.

If you want to catch a wave, you've got to be in the right place, paddle hard and pop up at the right time. It takes learning, focus and effort.

To catch the wave of Conscious Capitalism, build a conscious business and cultivate flow and flourishing in your work does not happen by itself. You've got to show up - for yourselves, others and purpose - your own and that of your business.

"

That which we persist in doing becomes easier for us to do.
Not that the nature of the thing itself has changed
but our power to do it is increased.

~ Ralph Waldo Emerson

"

What You Can Do

Working for Good is a state of being, an orientation to doing and an approach to work and business in which the Process is the Product. How we show up makes the difference.

In this section of the book, we'll explore ways you can do the work to be the change!

Here are some of the ways you can begin or continue your journey.

1. Learn more.
2. Cultivate and care for yourself.
3. Connect with and care for others.
4. Find and follow your purpose and passion.
5. Put a flag in the ground. Stand for something.
6. Work with, buy from, invest in and otherwise engage with companies that deeply reflect the principles of Conscious Capitalism.
7. Activate your entrepreneurial spirit and start a conscious business. Create new products and services, and new ways of doing business that reflect and advance the principles of Conscious Capitalism.
8. Cultivate the skills of Working for Good and bring them to life in your work and business.

At the end of the book we provide references to resources for learning more. In the pages ahead we'll share some insights into caring for yourself and practicing the skills of Working for Good.

At the end of the day, you'll either be more or less engaged with the emerging Conscious Capitalism movement. It will happen with or without you. I can say from direct experience, it is a blast being purposefully engaged with the emergence!

We fail to realize that mastery is not about perfection. It's about a process, a journey. The master is the one who stays on the path day after day, year after year. The master is the one who is willing to try, and fail, and try again, for as long as he or she lives.

~ George Leonard

Maintaining Perspective

This can be the exciting and overwhelming part of the book and of your journey to engage with the emerging Conscious Capitalism movement and to embody the skills of Working for Good. Take a deep breath! And remember that life is a long distance journey, not a sprint.

You don't have to absorb and embody the ideas and practices that follow all at once. It is more likely that they will stick if you focus on one or two at a time, for days, even weeks. Then focus on another one or two.

And you don't resonate with any of the ideas or practices, just move past them until you find one that resonates, and focus on that.

This book and these practices are meant to be a refuge and support for you, not a burden. Remember the story of the Chinese farmer. We never quite know the outcomes of events or our actions. But we can observe what seems to be emerging and working well, and we can try it ourselves. If it works, we can stick with it and, perhaps, it will become part of who we are.

The exercises and practices that follow are designed to cultivate our ability to connect with our purpose, to sustain our passion, energy and health, to foster connection and collaboration with others, and, ultimately, to enhance our ability to be conscious and to show up for what is emerging in ways that foster flourishing for all.

Training partners and teams can be tremendously helpful, even essential, for learning any new skill. So invite others to join you or join others who are already engaged in practice.

At the end of the book we'll point you to some places you can go to find training partners and learning communities.

Love yourself first, and everything else falls in line.
You really have to love yourself to get
anything done in this world.

~ Lucille Ball

Care for Yourself

One of the key messages coming from many of the pioneers of Conscious Capitalism is that trust, love and care form the foundation of a healthy, thriving corporate culture and a sustainable conscious business.

Building a culture of trust, love and care begins with ourselves. If we treat ourselves with respect, then we can care for others. And to sustain the long term effort and engagement required to build anything durable and sustainable, we need the capacity and energy to persist, adapt, learn and grow.

When we are over-stressed and tapped out, our ability to show up with Conscious Awareness is diminished. When we are rested, nourished and healthy, we are better equipped to deal with the daily exigencies of life and work and can address challenges we face with clarity and expansiveness. We can be understanding and patient, with ourselves and others.

Being the change begins at home by caring for ourselves, and, from there, for others.

As countless successful Conscious Leaders will attest, you grow, your company grows. You stagnate, your company stagnates. Care for yourself in wholesome ways, you cultivate a culture of care. Disregard yourself, and you create an unhealthy culture.

In some ways, this may be the most essential to lesson learn and most difficult to fully embrace. But really, if you want to create a healthy conscious business, love yourself so you can love others.

66

We are what we repeatedly do.
Excellence, then, is not an act, but a habit.

~ Aristotle

The Process is the Product: Fuel for the journey

How do you start your day? What do you eat for breakfast? And what does this have to do with business? Well, what you eat effects how you feel, which affects how you behave, your energy level and clarity of thinking, among other things. If you are going to show up at your best, then treat yourself with care and respect, and nourish you mind/body/spirit with good clean fuel. Here's the basic smoothie recipe I use to start my day:

- One avocado (including the seed!)
- One banana
- Two dates
- A handful of kale (always) and sometimes other greens
- One scoop of raw cacao powder
- One scoop of Tonic Alchemy micro-nutrient formula
- One scoop of Chia seed (or other fibre - flax, psyllium, etc.)
- Papaya and/or other fruit
- Berries, nectarines, etc. as they are in season. All organically grown.
- A chunk of raw ginger.
- A couple dashes of cayenne chili powder.
- Coconut water
- Two scoops of steel cut oats (soaked in water overnight)
- Sometimes I add acai powder or frozen acai

The whole thing is about 800 calories. I can drink this at 6:00 am, go through a full morning, work out at noon, then eat lunch at 2 pm. You don't have to drink what I do, but I encourage you to think about what you eat and drink – recognizing that it is fuel that brings energy, vitality and awareness to work.

"An ounce of practice is worth a ton of theory."

~ Anonymous Taoist Master

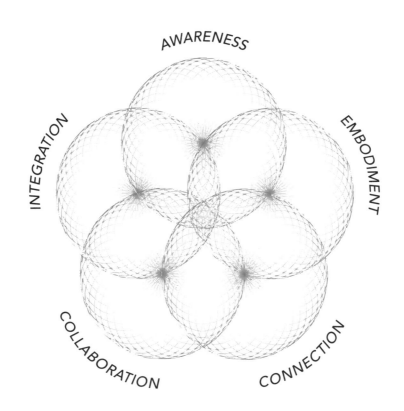

PRACTICES

Adapting to change and keeping pace with an emerging movement requires that we continually expand our capabilities, elevate existing skills and learn new ones. Turning capacities into skills and becoming more skilful requires practice. Practice rocks!

When we aspire to mastery and passionately pursue proficiency, diligently repeating exercises to develop our understanding and skill, we stretch and transform ourselves. Learning is living! Moving from deep within, informs how we move in the world.

Focusing our practice on the five skills of Working for Good prepares us – individually and together - to embody the principles of Conscious Capitalism. The five skills are:

- **Awareness**: The skill that enhances all other skills.
- **Embodiment**: Moving with awareness, into action.
- **Connection**: Engaging with others, with awareness, to move together.
- **Collaboration**: Focusing our attention and energy to co-create with others.
- **Integration**: Recognizing our on-going emergence, seeing our edges and holes, cultivating new levels of awareness and being.

On the following pages you will find exercises you can employ to cultivate the skills of Working for Good. The higher the quality of the practice, the better prepared we are to face challenging situations and whatever life presents.

A few recommendations: Use everything you've got. Your capacities for sensing, feeling, thinking and reflecting are all essential. Recognize emerging process - catch the wave, connect with flow. Nothing feels better than a good ride. Stay loose! Flexibility is key to successful adaption and, thus, for surviving, propagating and flourishing.

Between stimulus and response, there is a space.
In that space lies our freedom and power to choose our response.
In our response lies our growth and freedom.

~ Viktor Frankl

The Process is the Product
Awareness Practice: Tuning In

Tuning in is a process of noticing what is going on within ourselves, with others and around us. We can tune in to body sensations and processes - like our breath, to emotions, to thoughts, to what is going on around us and to any combination of these. Here's a taste of body scanning.

Sit or stand in a comfortable position. If you'd like, close your eyes (after your read the rest of the instructions!). Notice your feet on the floor. Notice the quality of your breath. Is it deep or shallow? Is it quick or slow. Take a few deep, purposeful breaths, as you exhale allow your shoulders to drop.

Now focus your attention to the top of your head, and allow it to slowly move down your body, all the way to your feet. Continue to breathe as you move your attention. Notice any sensations or tension calling for attention along the way. When you do, just notice, breathe and move on. When you are ready, take another deep breath or two, open your eyes.

Did you notice anything you hadn't noticed before? Did you find any tension in your body? Notice anything else? We can do the same thing with thoughts and feelings, and invariably find things we hadn't noticed before focusing our attention in this way.

Observe yourself at work (with whatever frequency and duration you choose) and recognize what is going on inside that you may not be aware of. For instance, sitting at your desk or in a meeting, tune into your body, recognize how you are breathing, observe any sensation in your body, notice thoughts or feelings that may be floating under the surface. Just that. Just observe, notice and move on.

"

When you look into a pool of water,
if the water is still,
you can see the moon reflected.

If the water is agitated,
the moon is fragmented and scattered.
It's harder to see the true moon.

Our minds are like that.
When our minds are agitated,
we cannot see the true world.

~ Traditional Zen saying

"

The Process is the Product
Awareness Practice: Reflection

"How's it going?" "What is working well?" "What are opportunities for improvement?" "What have I learned from this passage?" "What new approaches might we explore?" "What skills can we develop to be better prepared for similar circumstances?" "How do I feel about this process?" "What might those feelings indicate?"

These are a few of countless questions we can ask ourselves as we hold up figurative mirrors for ourselves and each other to reflect on the process, status and outcomes of our endeavors. Reflection is a uniquely human attribute and an integral element in our ongoing learning, growth and development.

Much as a dancer uses a mirror to reflect the precision of her movement and to facilitate refinement, we can use the reflective capacity of our minds and feedback from others, to clarify and deepen understanding, facilitate refinement of our orientation to people, processes and challenges. Examples of Reflection practices include writing in a journal or debriefing with others after a conversation, meeting or other experience.

At the end of every day I reflect on the events of the day and their implications. I tune into the status of my various projects (including personal development, physical fitness etc.) and the experiences and issues in my core relationships. Every week I write at least one blog post, which is always in part a reflection on an issue or topic relevant to my work and life. Every month I write a newsletter called Reflections, which provides a monthly pause to look back and ahead, and to sense how it all comes together for me right now.

How do you reflect?

Movement is a medicine for creating change in a person's physical, emotional, and mental states.

~ Carol Welch

The Process is the Product
Embodiment Practice: Move!

Movement is life. And life is movement. If we are going to be vital, alive and healthy, if we are going to engage with the emerging Conscious Capitalism movement, we've got to move!

Some of the benefits of moving our bodies...

- Gets circulation going
- Oxygenates the blood
- Releases endorphins and enhances our mood
- Boosts energy
- Feels good
- Shifts our perspective and opens space for creativity to flow
- Takes us from one place to another
- And so much more...

Awareness begets awareness, and movement begets movement. Yes, we can overdo it, but consistent, healthy movement increases our ability to keep moving.

When we move our bodies, our whole being moves.

When we move with others, we do more than traverse terrain together. We share the experience and energy of moving, which can transfer to moving together in our work.

If you want to build a healthy, dynamic team and a life-enhancing business, think of your body as a metaphor. Move with passion, purpose, energy, enthusiasm and awareness.

"

Follow your bliss!

~ Joseph Campbell

The Process is the Product
Embodiment Practice: What's Your Why?

Tune in to your breath and body as you reflect on the question: What beliefs form the foundation of your orientation to work or to your business? And write them down.

Now reflect on this question and write down your response to it: What do I do? Spend some time with it. Describe what you do in some detail, including for whom you do it.

Now address this question and write your answer succinctly: Why do I do that?

Now reflect on your response, answer it again, succinctly: Why do I do that?

And reflect on the last answer and ask yourself again: Why do I do that?

One more time: Why do I do that?

Now look back at all of your responses and find the pieces that fit together to describe your core purpose. Once you have done this, take time to distill it down to the shortest statement that captures the essence of your purpose. As stated earlier, the purpose, the "Why" of Working for Good is: **Working for Good exists to foster flourishing**.

Live with it. Reflect on it. See how your body responds to it. Share it with others.

When it feels true and grounded, begin to use it to orient yourself, your work, your business. Explore how your "Why" informs what you do and how you do it, how it guides your decisions and the way you relate to your stakeholders. And revisit it from time to time, as Tony Hsieh and Zappos continue to do.

"

Individual commitment to a group effort --
that is what makes a team work, a company work,
a society work, a civilization work.

~ Vince Lombardi

"

The Process is the Product
Embodiment Practice: Commitment

Reflect on and respond to the following questions:

What commitments do you make with respect to yourself?

- Will you allow yourself the time to check in with yourself?
- How will you take care of yourself?
- How will you develop a supportive environment and network for yourself?

What principles guide your behavior?

- How will you monitor your words and actions?
- How will you respond when you find you are contradicting your principles?

What commitments do you make with respect to your relationships with your colleagues and team members?

- How will you communicate with each other?
- What supportive patterns and practices will you develop and apply?
- How will you hold each other accountable to your commitments?

What commitments do you make with respect to your relationships with other stakeholders?

- How will you establish and sustain accountability in your relationships with them?

"

To be with another in this way means that for the time being, you lay aside your own views and values in order to enter another's world without being prejudiced. In some sense it means that you lay aside your self; this can only be done by persons who are secure enough in themselves that they know they will not get lost in the world of the other, and that they can comfortably return to their own world when they wish.

~ Carl Rogers

"

The Process is the Product
Connection Practice: Deep Listening

Let's begin by tuning in, with awareness. Get into a comfortable position and take a few breaths. Relax your jaw and shoulders. Breathe as you feel your spine lengthen. Continue to breathe as you move through the exercise.

Imagine you are with someone you work with who is difficult for you. Perhaps you have different opinions, or you do things differently, or you are competitive with each other. In any case, you are called upon to make a decision together. What do you do?

Step one: Observe judgment. As you engage with this person, notice any judgments that come up for you. Hear the voice in your head telling you its stories about this person and his or her ideas.

Step two: Suspend judgment. Even if you are right, let it go. You don't have to let it go forever or lose whatever truth may be in your stories, but put them aside for now. Totally.

Step three: Inquiry. Ask yourself questions about this person and her perspective. Where is she coming from? Why might she think the way she does? How might your behavior influence the way she thinks and acts? Ask her meaningful questions to draw out authentic answers that can help you to understand her and her perspective. Really listen to her responses.

Envision opportunities you have to apply this in your work in the face of a challenging person or situation. And go for it!

We don't see things as they are,
we see them as we are.

~ Anais Nin

The Process is the Product
Connection Practice: Our Relationship to Others

Take a few breaths. Feel your body. Move a little bit. Anything up for you? Observe it until it passes (unless you need to deal with it) and then read on.

Imagine you are making a business call to an important client or colleague. Her assistant answers the phone.

How do you greet him? What is your experience of him? Do a quick body scan or an emotional body scan or a scan of your thoughts. What do you find?

Now imagine you are talking with the client or colleague you called. How do you greet her? What is your experience of her? Do a quick body scan or an emotional body scan or a scan of your thoughts. (See page 77 for the Tuning In exercise) What do you find?

What are the differences between the way you greeted and related to the assistant and the person you called to talk with? How do these difference reflect any biases or patterns you have in relation to one or both of them?

Now imagine you are on the phone with someone else, having an uncomfortable conversation. What is your last thought as you hang up? How does that last instant feel to you? Notice and describe any body sensations that accompany that last instant.

Our relationships with others are colored by an infinite variety of factors, including our biases and past experiences. If we recognize how we relate and respond to others, our orientation may shift if it is not aligned with our intentions and commitments.

No one can whistle a symphony.
It takes a whole orchestra to play it.

~ H. E. Luccock

The Process is the Product
Collaboration Practice: Facilitation

Facilitate means "to make easy." Facilitation is the art and practice of making collaboration easy (or easier), and facilitative behaviors foster ease of movement through even the most challenging passages. Good facilitation is like a hot knife through butter.

Facilitation presupposes our intention to collaborate, our interest in doing so without getting mired in conflict, and our commitment to authentic relationship and individual and collective growth.

Facilitation catalyzes the wisdom of the group and fosters decisions that engage the hearts and minds of all involved in order to generate unified action.

Here are some facilitative behaviors to foster the flow of collaboration.

- Set the context for conversations.
- Tune in to see how we are feeling and if there is anything taking our attention.
- Check in with one another to ensure that we are on the same page.
- Suspend judgments and practice deep listening.
- Establish clearly defined roles, responsibilities and decision-making processes.
- Ask clarifying questions if we don't understand something.
- Reinforce ground rules and agreements set to guide the collaboration.
- Slow down or, sometimes, speed up!

We can embody facilitative behaviors whether we are serving as a facilitator or participant in a conversation, meeting or ongoing collaboration.

> *A man cannot do right in one department of life whilst he is occupied in doing wrong in any other department. Life is one invisible whole.*
>
> *~ Mahatma Gandhi*

Integration

Integration happens. Truly. If we are alive – learning, growing, developing, engaging with life with Conscious Awareness and practicing the other skills of Working for Good, integration happens.

We find ourselves with deeper understanding and an expanded perspective, greater and more fully embodied awareness, healthier relationships and more fruitful and flowing collaboration. Old patterns restricting our vision and flow seem to loosen or disappear, and we may notice or sense new edges and opportunities for learning, growth and development.

While integration happens on its own, we can cultivate it by…

- Slowing down and taking time for reflection
- Asking probing questions
- Asking others for their feedback or reflections
- Looking for and recognizing repeating patterns in our story or history – issues or challenges that seem to come up over and over
- Moving with awareness – that is, doing any or all of the above while you are moving!

As we integrate, we become ourselves more fully, immersed in a virtuous cycle. Our relationship to practice and the work of becoming the change shifts to a place where it just is. Maybe there is effort, maybe there isn't. In some respects, it is all the same. We become the emergence, as we recognize that all there is, is emergence.

I slept and dreamt that life was joy.
I awoke and saw that life was service.
I acted and beheld that service was joy.

~ Rabindranath Tagore

Closing Reflections

On some innate human level, we are called to move towards improvement - to increase our chances for individual and collective survival, and to elevate the quality of our experience of life. Most of this movement happens "under the hood," below or beyond the view of our Conscious Awareness.

Yet, apparently, the more Conscious Awareness comes online, the more effective, efficiently, creatively things work under the hood.

Perhaps the most profound thing you can do to more deeply connect with the emerging wave of Conscious Capitalism and with your own flow in relation to it, is to reflect; to recognize the signs within and around you that guide you to a certain way of orienting and being.

Something magnificent is emerging for humanity. What exactly it is and where it will lead is truly a mystery. But as we develop an embodied understanding of inter-connectedness and the human foundations of business, perhaps the emergence becomes more manifest, more tangible.

As our awareness expands and our hearts open, work truly becomes love made visible and business becomes a powerful force for elevating humanity and fostering flourishing.

Welcome to the movement! May it move through you, with you and within you.

 RESOURCES

On the pages to follow you will find references to resources in the Working for Good and Conscious Capitalism ecosystems.

These web sites can connect you to more information on the ideas represented in this book and to the resources outlined on the following pages.

WorkingforGood.com is our principal site, which provides access to our services and publications, as well as to our courses and radio program at entheos.com. You will find access to many other resources via WorkingforGood.com.

ConsciousCapitalism.org is the global hub of the Conscious Capitalism movement, providing access to information, resources and Conscious Capitalism events, as well as to conversation and community, both on-line and off-line.

BeingHuman.org is a web-based magazine and community exploring the human underpinnings of Conscious Capitalism from the perspective of science and philosophy.

Making a Difference
While Making a Living

WORKING
for GOOD

Jeff Klein

"In the new business paradigm, which manages for positive outcomes for all stakeholders, bringing your best self into the workplace is critical for individual, team, and business success. Jeff Klein's insightful book makes remarkable use of story and guided reflections to provide readers with insights on how to uncover one's best self and help co-create businesses where everyone flourishes."

~ John Mackey, co-CEO, Whole Foods Market

Working for Good: Making a Difference While Making a Living is a practical guidebook for becoming a conscious entrepreneur, intrapreneur or change agent at work. It is designed to inspire, inform, engage, activate and assist readers in their pursuit of building and operating conscious enterprises.

Working for Good delves more deeply into the essential skills outlined in **It's Just Good Business.**

When read and discussed together by team members, alliance partners and other collaborators, Working for Good fosters deeper awareness, connection and collaboration.

Working for Good has received the following awards:

2010 Gold Nautilus Award – Conscious Business/Leadership
2010 Bronze Axiom Business Book Award – Entrepreneurship
2010 Bronze Independent Publisher Book Awards – Business/Career

Visit **WorkingforGood.com** to order Working for Good. For bulk orders, contact service@workingforgood.com.

IT'S JUST
GOOD BUSINESS™

WITH JEFF KLEIN

Join award-winning author Jeff Klein and his guests to explore the power of Conscious Capitalism® and the practice of Working for Good.®

en＊theosRadio

THE PRACTICE OF
WORKING FOR GOOD

WITH JEFF KLEIN

A 4-week course to cultivate skills for becoming the change you want to see in the world.

en＊theosAcademy

IT'S JUST
GOOD BUSINESS™
WITH JEFF KLEIN

A 6-week course on the power of Conscious Capitalism and the practice of Working for Good.

en＊theosAcademy

IT'S JUST
GOOD BUSINESS

JEFF KLEIN

Blissitations
Get Your Meditation On!

Working for Good & It's Just Good Business @entheos.com

Telecourses

The Practice of Working for Good: A four-week course of practice, cultivating skills for becoming the change you want to see in the world. Three twenty-minute sessions per week.

It's Just Good Business: A six-week introduction to Conscious Capitalism and Working for Good. One sixty-minute class per week.

Recorded "Blissitation"

It's Just Good Business: A fifteen-minute guided meditation focusing on our attention on purpose, inter-connectedness, the emergence of Conscious Capitalism and the practice of Working for Good. A great way to start the day or to refocus during trying times.

Radio Program

It's Just Good Business: Join Jeff Klein and his guests – pioneering servant leaders and inspiring innovators – to explore the power of Conscious Capitalism and the practice of Working for Good. Through their stories and best practices, you'll deepen your understanding of how to create more resilient, sustainable and life-enhancing businesses that serve a higher purpose and create value for all of their stakeholders.

You can access all of these resources via **WorkingforGood.com**.

LIBERATING THE
HEROIC SPIRIT OF BUSINESS

CONSCIOUS
CAPITALISM

FOREWORD BY BILL GEORGE

JOHN MACKEY
Co-CEO, Whole Foods Market

RAJ SISODIA

HARVARD BUSINESS REVIEW PRESS

John and Raj provide a deep dive into the emergence of Conscious Capitalism in this epic book published by Harvard Business Review Press. (hbr.org)

From the book promotional copy:

> There's a new business revolution brewing… don't let your organization miss out. Whole Foods, Trader Joe's, Wegmans, Costco, The Container Store. You shop there not only for the products they sell but also for the business philosophy these market leaders are pioneering.
>
> In Conscious Capitalism, iconic CEO John Mackey and professor Raj Sisodia show how such companies like Whole Foods Market, Trader Joe's, Wegmans, Costco, and The Container Store are creating a movement that's transforming business. The authors present the fundamental principles and practices of their bold new vision of Conscious Capitalism: businesses operating from a sense of higher purpose and prospering financially, while also generating other critical forms of value — emotional, social, intellectual, ecological, financial, and spiritual. These are businesses built on love and care instead of fear and stress.
>
> Some of today's best companies — Google, UPS, Southwest Airlines, Bright Horizons, Patagonia, Panera, Starbucks, REI, and others —are making this vision real. They're full-throated advocates for free markets, entrepreneurship, competition, and property rights. But they operate by a markedly different set of principles.
>
> Drawing on decades of personal experience and interviews and authored by the high-profile leaders of the movement, this revolutionary book gives leaders in every industry and sector a blueprint for much-needed change.

Highly recommended reading for anyone who wants to immerse themselves in the philosophy of Conscious Capitalism and great stories of its emergence and application.

 APPRECIATIONS

While I would need another book to thank everyone who contributed to the process of manifesting this book, I will take the risk of calling out a handful. Thanks to...

My daughter Meryl Fé for informing, inspiring and putting up with me.

Peter Baumann for holding a vast space for Being Human.

Doug Rauch for embodying the essence of Conscious Capitalism and for being such a great collaboration partner.

Julie van Amerongen for being an unwavering example of loyalty, steadfastness, gracious service and impeccable collaboration.

John Mackey for continually blazing new trails and for living his commitment to freedom and flourishing.

Doug Levy, Rand Stagen, Cheryl Rosner, Rick Voirin, Carrie Freeman-Parsons and the rest of the Conscious Capitalism, Inc. trustees for being a great expedition team and for creating a powerful container for the emergence of Conscious Capitalism.

Brian Johnson, John Carey and the en*theos team for always inspiring excellence.

Soul surfer Garth Murphy for being a master guide on my ever-deepening dance with the waves and exploration of ecosystems.

Mikyo Riggs and the Marin MMA team for being master teachers and learning partners.

DJ Grimes for his inspired design and delivery under pressure. Scott McIntosh for his insightful comments and suggestions, and his enthusiastic support. Andrea Yallop for her enduring friendship. All my family, friends, clients, collaborators and teachers.

 USE OF PROCEEDS

As a reflection of our recognition of inter-connectedness and interdependence, and in keeping with our commitment to create value for all of our stakeholders, we are contributing a portion of the proceeds from the sale of *It's Just Good Business* to Conscious Capitalism, Inc. and the Self-Help Initiative for Sustainable Development, in Liberia, West Africa.

We invite and encourage you to join us in supporting these organizations.

Conscious Capitalism, Inc. is the principle organization cultivating and propagating the philosophy of Conscious Capitalism – providing learning resources and facilitating communities of inquiry through publications, chapters, executive roundtables and events for a variety of audiences. **ConsciousCapitalism.org**

The Self-Help Initiative for Sustainable Development exists to reduce social causes of poverty through access to education and economic empowerment. SHIFSD works for an empowered West African Community where all people enjoy sustainable peace and development. Jeremiah T. Burgess and the SHIFSD team embody a deep sense of purpose and passion, and persist with energy and optimism in the face of great, ongoing adversity. In the spirit of giving a "hand up, rather than a hand out," they support local students and entrepreneurs with training, coaching, access to information and other resources. Similarly, we support them with our expertise, information and guidance, as much as if not more than our funds. You can join us to do both – provide funds and other resources. **SHIFSD.org**

Affiliate Opportunity

You can support these organizations, yourself and us by selling copies of this book. Visit **WorkingforGood.com** to become an affiliate.

About Jeff Klein

Family: Animalia
Class: Mammalia
Species: *Homo sapiens*
Sex: Male
Biological role: Father to a teenage daughter

Purpose: Working for Good
Passions: Surfing, Brazilian Jiu-Jitsu, moving in general

Social/Business roles: Activator, Author, Producer & Process Facilitator

Current Tribal Connections

Working for Good: Chief Activation Officer & CEO of virtual, networked service agency

BeingHuman.org: Executive director & executive producer of Being Human events

Conscious Capitalism, Inc.: Trustee, executive team member & event producer

Entheos Enterprises: Academy faculty member, radio program host

SelfOptima: Director

Conscious Leader Network: Advisor

Self-Help Initiative for Sustainable Development (Liberia): Advisor